by **MICHAEL HARREN**

Introduction by **ADAM FITZGERALD**
Photography by **LUKE KURTIS**

Tentative Armor by Michael Harren was originally performed as a staged reading at Judson Memorial Church in Greenwich Village on 17 April 2013 and 28 October 2013. A full production followed at Dixon Place on 19 March 2014.

This book and the *Tentative Armor* album were made possible in part by the generous support of Roberto Cervantes, James Harren, and Jeanie Powell

Published by bd-studios.com, 2014

Copyright © 2014 Michael Harren
Some Rights Reserved
Tentative Armor is licensed under a Creative Commons Attribution-NonCommercial-ShareAlike 3.0 Unported License http://creativecommons.org/licenses/by-nc-sa/3.0/

© creative commons

All photography copyright © by luke kurtis except as noted below:
Photos by Michael Harren — 6, 53, 64
Pages from Michael Harren's subway notebook — 12, 64
Stills from performance video by Blake Drummond — 16-25, 30
Stills from "Go." music video by Blake Drummond — 55-63
Photo of 17 April 2013 *Tentative Armor* performance by Micah Bucey — 68

Art Direction and Design by luke kurtis
Cover design by John Ong
Cover photo by Ben Strothman
Editorial and creative consulting by Steven Klapow

Print ISBN 978-0-9890266-3-5
eBook ISBN 978-0-9890266-5-9

bd-studios.com
New York, NY

CONTENTS

Preface — 7

Introduction — 9

Shadowing I — 13

Dream I — 16

Polly Put The Kettle On — 17

Mango — 24

Shadowing II — 27

Dream II — 30

When It Will Bloom — 31

Shadowing III — 37

Dream III — 38

Five Tasks of Grief — 40

Go. — 54

Shadowing IV — 65

Invocation — 66

PREFACE

by MICHAEL HARREN

In August of 2012 I returned to New York City in a haze of grief after having spent the previous four weeks in Prescott Valley, Arizona caring for my mother as she was dying of lung cancer and then clearing out her apartment after she passed. The simple question "Now what?" reverberated in my head as I came back to my previous life with a completely new reality and sense of my own mortality.

Truly, everything shifted and I became desperately aware that my time on this planet had its own expiration date. Somehow, I managed to turn the pain and regret into a need for momentum with my creative life. My mother had been a champion of my music-making for my entire life, and this was the best way I could think of to honor her memory.

Enter Judson Community Church's Art's Minister, Micah Bucey. My good friend Ken Kidd had nudged me toward Micah back in May 2012 after we'd attended a brilliant performance of Steven Stratford's *Methtacular!* Really, Ken's words were probably something like, "Go talk to Micah *now* about doing your show at Judson. I'll wait outside." Ken has a way of shutting up my naysaying, and for that, I am so thankful. I introduced myself to Micah and stammered out a self-deprecating description of this little idea I had, and Micah said, "That sounds great; let's have coffee."

Micah and I didn't get around to having our coffee date until after I returned from my time with my mom, but we finally made it happen. Over coffee, I told him of my still vague plan to combine stories with electronic and orchestral instruments. No matter how many reasons I tried to give him to tell me this was impossible, his responses were increasingly enthusiastic.

"I don't even know what this show is about."
"Yes."
"There will be some extremely adult material. Is that okay?"
"Yes!"
"I barely have anything written, nor a plan for what I will be writing about!"
"YES!"

So, we set a date, and I set to writing. I asked the brilliant Adam Fitzgerald to direct (yes!), recruited Leah Coloff and David Packer to play cello and viola (yes! yes!) and, next thing you know, I am premiering this strange collection of stories and sounds to a packed room in a historic church in New York City's West Village.

More and more yeses followed that glorious night, which lead to another reading of the show with an additional musician, Gabryel Smith on violin, which then led to a full theatrical performance of the show at another historical New York landmark, Dixon Place.

This brings us to the pages of this book, lovingly assembled by my friend and colleague luke kurtis, wrapped in a cover by John Ong and Ben Strothmann, and chock full of stills from Blake Drummond's dazzling videography. I am overwhelmed with gratitude for the kind spirits who have appeared during the course of this project.

This process taught me how to make something positive out of the overwhelming grief I felt from losing my mother. It taught me that I am an artist. But, above all else, it taught me how to say 'yes.'

Thank you for sharing in my work.

Love,

Michael Harren

INTRODUCTION
by ADAM FITZGERALD

Dear Reader,

I was honored and thrilled when Michael asked me to direct this show. Working with Michael to mount *Tentative Armor* was a bizarre, wonderful and unique experience, and one that I can say I truly loved. I often felt like I had been let in on a beautiful secret, and asked to help Michael share that secret with the world in a way that would, hopefully, sort of, make sense.

At any moment during the rehearsal process, you might have found us trying to figure out the best use of Michael's bum for a kiddie-poop joke, or we could be discussing stage imagery for messages from the Great Beyond, the Universe, God, or (as we had dubbed them) the *Lady Voices*. Before we began this journey, I had no idea what I was getting into, so I feel it is only fair to prepare you before you turn the first pages of this book. Lest you be confused, expecting a recap of a "normal" night of performance, I will share with you an actual text-message exchange between Michael and me, perhaps two days before we arrived at the theatre:

Adam: Random, but is there a particular color you associate with the voices?
Michael: Which voices? The God voices?
A: Yes.
M: I was thinking green or orange, but I just looked up the color for the crown chakra—it's violet.
A: Okay I like violet. I was thinking blue, but violet seems better.

The show is part music, part performance art, part acting, part storytelling, part orchestration, part comedy, part embarrassing anecdotes, part (more) music, and all heart. Every moment—from the subtly touching and honest to

the crass and sexual—comes from a place of truth. There are few artists out there presenting their work with such a wonderful mix of courage and care, with a never-ending eye toward giving the audience a wonderful experience and a sublime uniqueness of voice. I hope, as you flip through these images and words, you enjoy this experience as much as I enjoyed helping Michael create it.

We all wear armor. Most of us present it as if it is the truth. Michael's is tentative, and he admits to his hesitation. He questions the validity of that which covers him, and it has made for a stunning evening in the theatre.

With all my best,

Adam Fitzgerald
Director

No one encapsulates my [?]
single dude ang[?]
And with en[ough?]
G is that "more"
like he does

ODE r LOUIS C[?]

Louis, I'm ridin[?]
Maybe you were here
  Then —
 Here —
This same seat and this plain
  here
And what a gift, I mean, to
Be here
in NYC
EN WHY CEE
Its this where I thought it would
be so
Glamorous
  Somehow

SHADOWING I

What a gift to be riding on the subway in New York City.
Writing on the subway
Scribbling words but
somehow it's still just me acting as if
pretending is the only step to becoming a New York Artist.
I cast a meager shadow
by hiding inside of yours.
Shadowing.

The men are hotter here in New York
Hotter than the guys I saw from my car in Houston, anyway,
and there was less chance for that stolen moment
of accidental intimacy… you know
brushing past a tank-topped sweaty bicep while boarding the train,
or a picture taken in secret with my iPhone.
I got pretty good at that before it started making me feel…
Dirty.
Like a digital rapist.

I know, they're just photos, and I never jerked off to them or anything, but… taking a picture of a hot guy on the subway instead of just saying hello is a little
sad—
Shadowing.

DREAM I

I'm walking through the city with him. We're trying to get somewhere yet unnamed but there's not much light on the streets, so I can't tell if cars are coming or if they're in the distance. He runs across the street and I'm left standing on the median, afraid of the oncoming cars. Each time I hesitate, I realize that I've just been afraid of a reflection and the car is really far away. I see him running off into the distance, unaware that I've stopped in the street.

POLLY PUT THE KETTLE ON

So, this isn't my day job. All this singing and writing and arting around and all. No. During the day, you can find me with this guitar—singing and dancing around with Brooklyn's snottiest, drooliest, fat baby bastards. The pre-school set. Park Slope's resident baby Jesus…'s. Babies Jesus?

(singing) Polly
Polly put the kettle on
Polly put the kettle on
We'll all have tea

Anyway, I first started this type of gig back in Houston in the late '90's. Around the same time I was discovering my computer as in home glory-hole via AOLs super-classy M4M chat rooms, I started teaching music at a Catholic Montessori school. I was so excited to be graduating from my previous career of waiting tables that it didn't dawn on me that a Catholic school may not so be hip on the idea of having a promiscuous cocksucker in their employ. I got a little paranoid.

Polly
Polly put the kettle on
Polly put the kettle on
We'll all have tea

And when I was singing with all these kids, my mind would sometimes… wander. At first it was a bit jarring to catch myself during a rousing chorus of "Wheels on the Bus" with a group of first graders wondering what the hell happened to that condom I used to fuck the guy I was holding in a headlock last night and forcing to say, "My name is Princess and I'm a sissy." I mean, it's not going to fall out of my pants leg when we get to the part about the mommies and daddies saying "I love you," is it?

Polly
Polly put the kettle on
Polly put the kettle on
We'll all have…

Does my beard still smell like ass and balls?

…tea

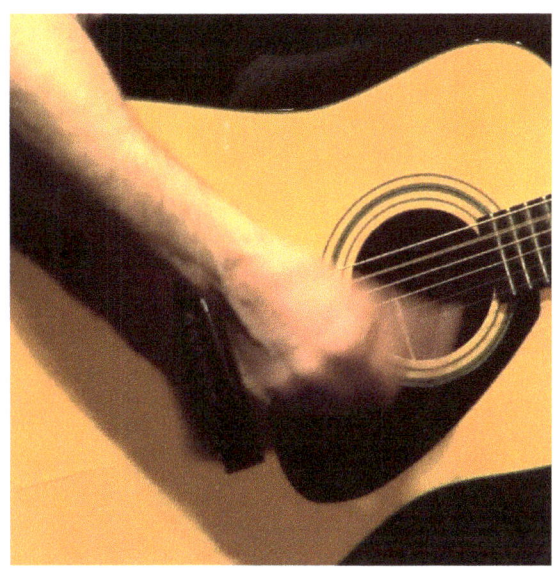

I knew hooking up on my way to class that morning wasn't the best idea. What the fuck? Even if I was still sporting eau du taint, it's not like a bunch of 7-year-olds could have identified the smell… Could they?

Start the fire and make the toast
Put the muffins down to roast
Set the table, you're the host
We'll all have tea

When I got to New York, I "graduated" to the infant/toddler set and found myself working at a high-end enrichment center on the Upper East Side—really an overblown babysitting service where toddlers could sit with their Caribbean nannies and listen to disgruntled musical theater wannabes resentfully sing songs at them while Mommy sees-and-bes-seen in the cafe downstairs. An interesting fact: In keeping with the commonly held belief that all men are potential child molesters, male teachers were not allowed to help the kids go to the bathroom.

Polly
Polly put the kettle on
Polly put the kettle on
We'll all have tea

My next New York job was as music teacher and assistant out in Brooklyn where I *was* required to help the kids with potty time, in spite of the fact that a parent pulled her kid from the school for fear a man—*me* specifically, 'cause I was the only one there—might change her daughter's diaper. The owner of the school had my back, but *come on*. Can you imagine where my head went? After the Catholic school fear-based teacher non-molestation workshops, the sexist bathrooms on the Upper East Side, and now the mom who was so afraid of my changing her daughter's shitty diaper that she sent her to another school.

So, I was terrified when I had to take little Henry to go potty. Just the two of us.

It wasn't my first time to take a kid to the shitter. In fact, earlier that week, this same kid totally pissed himself at the playground, and I walked the walk of self-pissing shame with him back to school and got him into clean clothes. So, we had a little bond, Henry and I. This was, however, my first number two.

So, Henry is sitting on the toilet, grimacing away, making it clear that we are indeed having a brown situation. So, in preparation, I pull some toilet paper off the roll, sort of bending awkwardly around him to get it. He finishes, gets up and then just kinda looks at me. It's clearly my move… but what's my move?

I reach out to hand the toilet paper to him, hoping to God that he takes it and wipes his own ass.

No dice.

Henry looks confused, and then casually turns around, pointing his shitty ass at me—his body language says, simply: "Clean it up, bitch."

In order to get down in it, I have to position myself between Henry and the open door to the bathroom, with my back to the door. While I'm cautiously cleaning up this kid's ass, I hear this little voice behind me:

"What are you doing to his butt, Michael?"

It's Phoebe, resident magical child and lover of unicorns and "nernaids." I don't know how long she's been there, but it's too long. Even though the clean up is nowhere near finished, I pull up Henry's pants and send him on his way, with the promise of a day graced with skid-marked Spiderman underpants.

Polly
Polly put the kettle on
Polly put the kettle on
We'll all have tea

I wanted to wrap up this story by telling you all what I learned that day. But the truth is, I didn't learn anything that day. Nor did I learn anything on the subsequent days of ass-wiping that followed, aside from the knowledge that I'd like to find another job that doesn't require wiping anyone's ass. But that's not the universal spirit message I was going for here.

Or, is it?

I am an ass-wiping, little-kid-teaching, music-writing, wrong-way-cyclist-hating, compulsively masturbating, piano-playing, perverted-sex-having *and avoiding*, sanctimonious, AND hugely loving, tofu-eating and omnivore-judging human who shits.

And has an occasional skid mark.

And that's how it is.

MANGO

In line at Whole Foods Union Square
My first summer in NYC
so, so alone
and…
Needing but not gonna say so
Even to my own heart

I'm standing in that line
One or two things in my hand
I don't remember what
Like I do this guy's arms
iPod strapped around his plump right bicep
Slightly flexed… he's holding a cup of fruit salad in his hand
My eye lands there right where the strap was
holding it back

I'm so captured… You know?

My awareness shifts
Reminding me that there is a person there
You know, attached to that plump bicep and hairy forearm

Sure enough
I look up and he's looking right into my eyes
Expressionless.
I mean
RIGHT into my eyes.

Is he pissed? In love?

A smile spreads across his face and he keeps looking into my eyes. Deep.

I whip out my phone and start faux texting, the only way I can think of to disappear without losing my place in line, and then glance back up and he's still looking into me. Like he had been looking into my eyes even when they were looking at the phone.

"Want some?"

"What?"

I see that the hand attached to the slighty hairy forearm attached to the plump, iPod strapped bicep attached to the guy in line next to me with the deeply looking

BEAUTIFUL

eyes is holding out that cup of fruit salad to me.

"Uh… Sure."

And I look at him. Strangely embarrassed that I don't have a fork.

"Just use your fingers"
"Okay"

I come back with a too-large cube of fruit that's hard to bite while hiding my imperfect teeth.

"Is that papaya?" I ask
"I think it's a mango."

I stumble out something about them being similar and he agrees.

His number is called and he heads to the register to pay for his fruit salad. I'm standing there hopeful and alone in this strange crowd of people.

He pays, picks up his remaining fruit, and heads out the door.

Without looking back.

SHADOWING II

But, there are moments of being alive and annoyed
But still a part of the city
That nodding head
Bobbing.
neck, spaghetti-ing.
The guy next to me is falling asleep on my shoulder
I'm half "COME ON" and half
"come on"
because, wouldn't it be nice to be a temporary pillow for a fellow traveller?
In the land of dating and connecting, I shadow, too
and a tiny ray of sunlight in the form of the bobble-headed gentleman sitting next to me
Why not?

DREAM II

Finally, I run across the street and catch up with him in the lobby of a small theater. I overhear another patron saying that they can't go in because the dress code for this show is a three-piece suit to keep everything feeling period. He buys the tickets anyway.

I excuse myself to find the bathroom, head down some stairs, past some children who were playing in the stairwell. "THIS IS NOT A PLAYGROUND," I yell as I pass through a door, not noticing the sign.

WHEN IT WILL BLOOM

The last time I fucked—I mean, *exclamation point* fucked—I was 26 years old and my life was playing the piano, fucking, and the fitness magazines I kept in my backpack along with scores from Bach, Barber, and Brahms, but their pages weren't as sticky. I was obsessed and thought I'd found a way to be whole by lifting, growing, consuming and imagining myself as a walking erect penis: veiny, red, and swollen. That's what he said anyway, but he didn't seem to mind when I was fucking him. On the days we aligned, we fucked.

Fucked.

I thought I was on top, and I was most of the time. He liked it that way—with my dick in his ass and his legs over my shoulders—but I was still worshiping him, and how hot I must have been to have a guy like that, right?

But, the last time I fucked (sans exclamation point, but chronologically correct), I'm standing in the bedroom of this bodybuilder-for-hire with $300 rolled up in my pocket. I'm 43 years old and I took the A train all the way to Harlem from Brooklyn, because that's how long its been, you know?

I notice my tendency to avert my eyes from my half of the wall of mirrors that make up his closet door. There's a light clamped to his dresser and he is posing in it. He doesn't mind that I'm only looking at him. That's what he's doing too. We're both trying to make me disappear in our own ways.

So, I am standing here with this massive guy flexing for me while I'm deliberately averting my eyes from my own reflection and wondering, "Can I stick it in him or is that extra?" When I asked in the e-mail, he just said, "$300 is for the time."

Whatever the fuck that means.

I lay on his bed (there's a towel there to protect the duvet), and he strokes my semi-flaccid cock with a most vacant, bored look on his face. I finally ask, or just say it, really: "I wanna fuck you."

He reaches over, opens the top drawer of his dresser and pulls out a condom, so I start playing with my dick, trying to get it hard, but it doesn't want to go there. We finally get the condom on, then he robotically stands up, spreads his legs apart and bends over, supporting his massive torso with his hands on the bed. Then he stands there waiting in the most clinical way, like he's waiting for a prostate exam.

Now, on my way here, I imagined how hot it would be to be owning this guy, or maybe God put me here so this guy could fall in love with me. I mean... that *is* where my mind goes. But now he's standing here in this most vulnerable of positions and willing to let me do whatever I want and my cock shrinks. This fucking Greek God is deigning to open up his asshole for me, and I am standing here—43, out of shape, a little flabby, droopy, and unable to look at myself. I start thinking, "Just get it in him! Get it hard and stick it in him, you fuckin' pussy!"

So, there he is bent over, legs spread. His face? Annoyance PLUS boredom, and I'm trying to shove a gummy worm into a keyhole.

After a few more minutes of this, I give up. I lay on his bed while he sits on top of me, flexing. I start jerking off until he takes over.

It takes forever.

Stroking.
Stroking.
Stroking.

And I'm still here
in this skin
waiting to get away.
While he reaches for more lube
I lay there awkwardly
wondering about love
and if it'll ever be my time
again.

He has to keep switching hands until I finally cum. Then he stands up and apologizes for applying hand sanitizer. I tell him I understand while I get dressed as fast as I can. It's freezing outside so I'm putting on layer after layer. It takes forever.

I head out to the subway in the hollow January streets of Harlem. The wind is beating my face while the trees stay eerily still, and I think about where I just was, where I was before that, and before that, still.

I see the glowing green of the subway station about a half block away, and the train is rumbling underfoot. I pick up my pace thinking, "There's no way I'll get on that train." While my feet fast and slow themselves ahead, I'm still thinking, "There'll be another train!'

I'm right outside the station now, and the train is pulling in, so I run to the stairs, imagining stumbling and smashing my face on the concrete floor. I keep running.

I hear the doors open as I reach the top of the stairs and try to descend through the sea of people exiting the train.

"Bing bong, stand clear of the closing doors, please."

As I jump down the last two stairs and dash a few more steps to the slowly closing doors and start to try to stop them with my hand and then pull back as if they'll eat me alive.

I stand there, looking through those windows at the people inside who made it:
Older
Younger
Some even look back at me with a distant sort of pity and I realize how badly I wanted to make it, and how I would have if I hadn't waited so long.

SHADOWING III

I'm here to write
Well, to get to my destination, but that feels secondary now
my pen scratching across the paper of this dollar ninety-nine notebook
and I'm thinking about my other shadow world
where ideas come and inspiration rises up and
beams like sunlight seen through shadowy trees
and somehow, lays on top of me in all its shimmer and glow
and slumbers thick in my neck and chest
waiting to be awakened, but layers and layers of these
and other regrets keep me here.

I was talking to a friend yesterday about the aftermath of the 9/11 attacks
And I found myself sad I wasn't living here yet.
Like the way I'm sad I never went on that date with Bryant
Or the way I never made it to Canada before David died,
though I thought of him every day before and have every day since.
the un-regretted regrets, so far unlain
my mother, my father, my sister, my brother
all alive and well, but I know I'm not the person I want to be to them
premeditated regret?
All the ways I watch myself be not enough for me
because it's easier to watch and listen, or hide and hope
in a pile of nothing but "almost" and "good enough."

(Michael and the audience hear a disembodied ancestral voice echo
from beyond. As if in a trance, he listens closely and repeats the words
that only he hears.)

This? This is?

Fuck "this."

(Michael exits the train.)

DREAM III

At the bottom of those stairs, I wander around many unmarked doors arranged in that perpetual circle that dreams do so well. I stumble upon a woman getting into costume for the show and realize I've wandered into the women's dressing room. I start backing out of the room, thinking she hasn't seen me.

"Oh, are you a pervert?" she asks seductively. "Is this what you're into?"

"No," I reply, "I'm really just lost down here. And, I'm queer so…"

She walks slowly toward me with that same seductive look on her face, puts her hand on mine and asks, "What kind of dreams do you hide from?"

And then I woke up.

FIVE TASKS OF GRIEF

I have on my refrigerator the most depressing piece of paper. It stays there fastened by four magnets - one on each corner, as if to say: "Yes, I want you and the ideas you represent in my life, but don't go flapping around and drawing attention to yourself every time I walk by."

The piece of paper is titled, "Five Tasks of Grief."

It arrived in a flurry of mailings from the hospice that helped me care for my mother during her last three weeks of her life. And while it took me a couple days to realize it, all this mail arrived right at the three month anniversary of my mother's death, so maybe this was some sort of "bereavement check-in" time. Which makes sense because the first morning that the mail started to arrive, I had been awakened by the sound of my deceased mother's voice calling my name in a half awake dream. I spent the first hour of that day sobbing in my bed, really unable (or unwilling, really) to move. You never know when these things are going to hit you. But I guess those hospice people do, because this piece of paper arrived just in time.

The page is arranged into two neat columns. One titled "Tasks of Grief," and the other, "Goals For Healthy Bereavement." I should stop here and mention how badly I'd like to mock this piece of paper with its airy-fairy language and guidance toward healing, but the truth is, this piece of paper kicks my ass every time I look at it. I mean, it fucking stings. So right when I want to crack a joke, my throat clenches up and the sides of my mouth force themselves down, my lip quivers, and it's to the couch or the floor or whatever is most convenient for a good sit-down with my feelings.

Now, I am the type of person who avoids these so-called "emotions" at all costs, though, as a child, my mother often reminded me that I was "different" and that I was "more sensitive" than the other kids. While that may have been a euphemism for "you will suck many cocks in your life," at the time it made me feel like she got me in a way that no one else did.

The call came on a Sunday night. It was really a text message from my brother. Even though all it said was "check your email," I knew. This is it.

6.20.2012

What made me grateful: We made it to Arizona today. Mom wouldn't answer the door, so my sister climbed the short fence and entered the apartment through the unlocked sliding door. Seeing my mother's skeletal silhouette in the doorway to her bedroom was… shocking. She's not well. Not well at all. But I'm so happy we are here for her.

6.21.2012

My brother arrived yesterday. His presence helped us over the hump of asking our mom some serious questions and getting all of us honest about what is really going on—she has a massive tumor on her lung. "Huge" was the word we read on the radiology report that lay abandoned on her kitchen table. The three of us sat in her room and told her that we wanted nothing but to help her in exactly the way she wanted to be helped.

TASK #1
TO ACCEPT THE REALITY OF THE LOSS

AUTO WRITING ON FIRST TASK OF GRIEF

#1 "To accept the reality of the loss"

a. "dealing with unfinished business
and acceptance before death"

Once my brothers and sisters and I were told there were only a few days to go I understood & accepted quite truth as in general when I could see that she was thin - like - concentration camp thin, and when we had insides hypnotist that called an oncologist on her table in dining room lung. HUGE. That's what it said.

What I didn't know about my mom (and there is a big part of me that kicks my ass for never asking - but what are regrets anyway?) was the close proximity of her friends.

Bonnie was my mom's best friend and it broke my heart each time she just

6.23.2012

Getting hospice set up for mom and how kind her doctor's assistant was with my brother and me. I've decided to stay as long as I can, in hopes that she can die at home in her own bed.

Being in the moment as best I can.

6.24.2012

Talking to my mom about what she wants us to do with her stuff when she's gone. This opened up the conversation about what she wants us to do with her body. This talk was so hard but my tears gave her the chance to mother me once more. I am so thankful for being on the other side of this conversation. It is such a relief to be perfectly current and not have to avoid saying what we both already know to be true: She is dying.

TASK #2
TO EXPERIENCE THE PAIN OF THE LOSS

I was crying so hard. She held my hand and said it's okay with a smile. She got to hug me one last time, and I got to hug her back, that's when I started to say goodbye.

2) To experience the pain of the loss:
The biggest feeling in all of this was of my broken relationship with my mother fading away. There was a time when I confided so many things in her — was it money that started to screw things up — when she co-signed on my car and she would end up having $300 to pay it off to stop the calls? There was a time after

6.28.2012

Mom had me show her best friend Bonnie each item in her closet to see if she wanted any of her clothes. Under ordinary circumstances this would have annoyed the crap out of me, but yesterday I was so happy and touched to be a part of this bittersweet exchange between my mom and her best friend.

I'm grateful for walking Bonnie back to her apartment with her bounty of clothes from my mom. She was so sad and started crying when I hugged her goodbye. A 40-year-old man and a 60-some-odd-year-old woman, crying in each others arms. Everything is so sad right now, but I'm still happy to be present.

TASK #3
TO ADJUST TO AN ENVIRONMENT IN WHICH THE DECEASED IS MISSING

7.3.12

I'm grateful for seeing Mom decline further. This feels like a terrible thing to say I am grateful for, but I know she is so unhappy living this way, and her steady decline means she might have some relief sooner rather than later.

I'm grateful for my friend Jeanie's advice to call hospice last night. I was freaking out, afraid I'd given mom too much morphine. The on-call nurse said, "At this point there are no mistakes. We just want her to be as comfortable as possible until it is time for her to go."

TASK #4
TO INTEGRATE THE MEANING OF THE LOSS INTO ONE'S LIFE

7.4.12

Waking up in the middle of the night to give medicine to mom and how it reminds me of the countless times she did the same for me. I don't wanna get all Elton John on you guys, but that's some Circle of Life shit right there.

How much mom's nurse loves her.

How much my mom's friends love her.

7.10.12

My mom has entered the final stage of life. The hospice nurse, Erika, described it as "a beautiful part of the process where she has one foot in each side." It was so interesting hearing her talk about death as "a beautiful process," and it helped me to realize that I feel the same way. As hard as it is for us here on the human side of things to say goodbye, I truly believe that my mom is going to be in a really cool new phase of her spirit's existence.

My friend Erin and I have changed the term "death rattle" to "heavenly huffs." Much nicer, right?

TASK #5
TO WITHDRAW EMOTIONAL ENERGY AND REINVEST IT IN ANOTHER RELATIONSHIP

7.11.12

My sweet mama passed away last night at 7:15. She went so peacefully, and she seemed to be comfortable in her last couple of days. I'm so happy she got to leave this world in exactly the way she wanted to.

That's all for today.

GO.

A separate page is the same page
With a different point of view
And isn't this the reason
For what we're going through?
We live a little
And love some more
And then we die
So here we are again, love
But what am I?
What am I?

Summer into autumn
Well, you know how that goes
In between we find a dream
And find out "letting go"
The seasons that enclose us in
The seasons outside those
They remain a mystery
In spite of what we know
In spite of what we think we know

Go
Wrap yourself in ether, sage and smoke
Go
You'll soar above the magpies and the oak
Go, go
Go, go

I'll keep you in my winter
My summer and my spring
I'll stay here and remember
When you were here with me
I'll live a little
And love some more
And then I'll die
And here we are again, love
Here am I
Here am I

Good.

It's the enemy of "the best" you know. And good is fine but is not extraordinary, or bold or shimmering or anywhere near what the universe or - I'll say it - God - wants from me and that's the truth and the slut. We ain't got no right to God there watch—
father, or
groovy gho—
and ask—
But tha—
you are —
you are s—
and hoping for me. And these — walls are holding this

SHADOWING IV

The "good" is the enemy of the best, you know.
And good is fine, but fine is not extraordinary
or bold and shimmering or anywhere near what the universe
or... I'll say it—what God wants from me.
Is God watching me like a disappointed parent,
head shaking and tsk-tsk-ing?

Maybe... but that's not all, right?
because you are God to me
and you are sitting here glowing and hoping for me to shimmer and quake
and these merciful walls hold up this omnipotent ceiling above
our heads and isn't this really God?
or me?

And, if I'm the God of tsk-tsking my own inaction,
then why don't I shut the fuck up and get to work?

INVOCATION

This.
This is.
This is here and
This.
This is.
This is here and this is
Free.

You may not know it yet
But these are your hands:
    Silver and forgotten.
And these are your feet:
    Calloused and golden.

And this is
All you anyway
And you are here to be.

You.
You are.
You are here and
You.
You are.
You are here and you are
Free.

PERFORMANCE HISTORY & CREDITS

17 and 18 SEPTEMBER 2010
"When It Will Bloom" performed at DiverseWorks, Houston, TX, for *Come As You Are: Houston!*
Curated by Chuck Jackson, Grayson Jacobs, and Blake Smith
Tech Director: Blake Smith
I played an early version of "When It Will Bloom" solo piano with a backing track I created with percussion and samples. This was the original version of the story, which stayed the same through the 2014 Dixon Place performance.

12 APRIL 2012
"Shadowing" performed at Dixon Place, New York City
I was one of several opening acts for *Gender Failure* by Ivan Coyote and Rae Spoon. Lauren Hunter and Mieke D also appeared that night.
Curated by Victoria Libertore
Production Manager: Rob Lariviere

17 APRIL 2013
Tentative Armor first public reading for Magic Time at Judson Memorial Church, New York City
Curated by Micah Bucey
Directed by Adam Fitzgerald
Tech Director: Zac Mosely
Videographer: Alison S.M. Kobayashi
Vegan food and literature: Rina Deych

Michael Harren - Piano, synthesizer, and laptop
Leah Coloff - Cello
David Packer - Viola

28 SEPTEMBER 2013
Tentative Armor second public reading at Judson Memorial Church, New York City
Directed by Adam Fitzgerald
Tech Director: Zac Mosely
Videographer: Alison S.M. Kobayashi
Sound: Eddie Sullivan
Vegan food and literature: Shoshanna Frishberg-Izzo

Michael Harren - Piano, synthesizer, guitar, and laptop
Leah Coloff - Cello
David Packer - Viola
Gabryel Smith - Violin

14 FEBRUARY 2014
"Mango" at The Parkside Lounge, New York City
New Work, New York curated by Gardiner Comfort
Michael Harren - Synthesizer and laptop

19 MARCH 2014
Tentative Armor premiere at Dixon Place, New York City
Directed by Adam Fitzgerald
Videographer: Blake Drummond
Production Manager: Rob Lariviere

Michael Harren - Piano, synthesizer, guitar and laptop
Leah Coloff - Cello
David Packer - Viola
Gabryel Smith - Violin

www.ingramcontent.com/pod-product-compliance
Lightning Source LLC
Chambersburg PA
CBHW061120010526
44112CB00024B/2922